God's Divine Provision

(31 Days Scriptural Declarations for Provision)

AF489175

Joy Mowete

God's Divine Provision

Visit the author at her website:
www.declarehisword.com

DEDICATION

I dedicate this book to our gorgeous son,
fumnanya –
who lives in prosperity and loves to buy
"so many things".

God's Divine Provision

IT IS WRITTEN

But He answered and said,
"It is written, 'Man shall not
live by bread alone, but by
every word that proceeds from
the mouth of God."
Matthew 4:4

The entrance of Your Words
gives light; It gives understanding
to the simple.
Psalm 119:130

God's Divine Provision

Introduction

The LORD is your Creator. Before He created you, He had already made provision for all your needs – both spiritual and physical (Psalm 139:13-18)

God's Divine Provision (31 Days Scriptural Declarations for Provision) is written to:

Help you trust and put all your faith in God.

Help you have an understanding and revelation of what the Word of God says in areas pertaining to all your needs.
Help you confess and pray with the Word of God.

Build a close relationship with God despite whatever is going on in your life or around you.

God has made you prosperous. Study His Word.

My prayer is that as you READ, CONFESS and PRAY with the Word of God in **God's Divine Provision** (31 Days Scriptural Declarations for Provision), you will have a revelation of God as JEHOVAH JIREH (THE LORD OUR PROVIDER), who is able to take care of all your needs both spiritual and physical in Jesus name. Amen.

DAY 1

1 Samuel 25:6
"And thus you shall say to him who lives in prosperity: "Peace be to you, peace to your house and peace to all that you have.

I declare and decree in the name of Jesus Christ,

The LORD is my Provider.

I live in prosperity.

I am prosperous in all my endeavors.

The peace of God is upon my life.

The peace of God is upon my household.

The peace of God is upon all that I have in Jesus name

God's Divine Provision

DAY
2

Haggai 2:19

"Is the seed still in the barn? As yet the vine, the fig tree, the pomegranate, and the olive tree have not yielded fruit. But from this day I will bless you."

I declare and decree in the name of Jesus Christ,

The LORD is my Provider.

Even when the seed is not yet in the barn.

Even when the vine, the fig tree, the pomegranate and the olive tree have not yet yielded fruit, from this day, the Almighty God will bless me.

I am blessed going out.

I am blessed coming in.

I am a channel of blessing.

I am highly favoured in Jesus name.

God's Divine Provision

DAY
3

Matthew 6:31-33

"Therefore do not worry, saying: 'What shall we eat?' or 'What shall we drink?' or 'What shall we wear?' For after all these things the Gentiles seek. For your heavenly Father knows that you need all these things. But seek first the kingdom of God and His righteousness and all these things shall be added to you.

I declare and decree in the name of Jesus Christ,

The LORD is my Provider.

I do not worry about what I will eat, what I will drink or what I will wear.

My heavenly Father knows that I need all these things.

I seek first the kingdom of God and His righteousness and all the things I need are given to me by my heavenly Father in Jesus name.

God's Divine Provision

DAY

4

Isaiah 1:19

"If you are willing and obedient, you shall eat the good of the land."

I declare and decree in the name of Jesus Christ,

The LORD is my Provider.

I am willing to serve and follow the LORD.

I am obedient (hearken, give ear, pay attention) to the commands of the LORD.

I eat the good of the land.

I am eating the good of the land.

I am blessed. I am a channel of blessing to the land in Jesus name.

God's Divine Provision

DAY
5

Hebrews 11:6

"But without faith it is impossible to please Him, for he who comes to God must believe that He is, and that He is a rewarder of those who diligently seek Him."

I declare and decree in the name of Jesus Christ,

The LORD is my Provider.

My faith is in God.

I believe you are the LORD God Almighty.

You are a rewarder of those who diligently seek you.

I am diligent in seeking the LORD.

The LORD will reward me in Jesus name.

DAY
6

John 15:5

"I am the vine, you are the branches. He who abides in Me, and I in him, bears much fruit, for without Me you can do nothing."

I declare and decree in the name of Jesus Christ,

The LORD is my Provider.

My Lord Jesus Christ is the vine and I am the branches.

I abide in Him (joined with Him) and He abides in me (joined with me)

I bear much fruit.

Without Jesus Christ, I can do nothing.

With Jesus Christ, I can do all things in Jesus name.

God's Divine Provision

DAY
7

Philippians 4:19-20
"And my God shall supply all your need according to His riches in glory by Christ Jesus. Now to our God and Father be glory forever and ever. Amen."

I declare and decree in the name of Jesus Christ,

The LORD is my Provider.

He is able, abundantly able to supply all my need according to His riches in glory by Christ Jesus.

To my God and Father, be all the glory forever and ever in Jesus name.

God's Divine Provision

DAY
8

Isaiah 58:11

"The LORD will guide you continually and satisfy your soul in drought and strengthen your bones. You shall be like a watered garden and like a spring of water whose waters do not fail."

I declare and decree in the name of Jesus Christ,

The LORD is my Provider.

The LORD will guide me continually.

He satisfies my soul in drought and strengthens my bones.

I am like a watered garden and a spring of water, whose waters do not fail in Jesus name.

God's Divine Provision

DAY
9

Genesis 39:2-3

"The LORD was with Joseph, and he was a successful man; and he was in the house of his master the Egyptian. And his master saw that the LORD was with him and that the LORD made all he did to prosper in his hand."

I declare and decree in the name of Jesus Christ,

The LORD is my Provider.

He is with me.

I am a successful man/woman.

I am successful in all that I do.

It is evident that the LORD is with me.

He makes the work of my hand to prosper in Jesus name.

God's Divine Provision

DAY
10

Hebrews 13:5-6

"Let your conduct be without covetousness: be content with such things as you have. For He Himself has said "I will never leave you nor for-sake you." So we may boldly say: "The LORD is my helper; I will not fear. What can man do to me?"

I declare and decree in the name of Jesus Christ,

The LORD is my Provider.

My conduct is without covetousness (not greedy.)

I am grateful to God for all that I have.

My God will never leave me nor forsake me.

I am not afraid. The LORD is my helper in Jesus name.

God's Divine Provision

DAY
11

Philippians 4:6

"Be anxious for nothing, but in everything by prayer and supplication, with thanksgiving, let your requests be made known to God."

I declare and decree in the name of Jesus Christ,

The LORD is my Provider.

I am anxious for nothing.

I am totally dependant on God.

He is faithful and liable.

In everything by prayer and supplication, with thanksgiving, I make my requests known to God in Jesus name.

God's Divine Provision

Jeremiah 17:7-8

"Blessed is the man who trusts in the LORD, and whose hope is the LORD. For he shall be like a tree planted by the waters, which spreads out its roots by the river, and will not fear when heat comes; but its leaf will be green, and will not be anxious in the year of drought nor will cease from yielding fruit."

I declare and decree in the name of Jesus Christ,

The LORD is my Provider.

I am blessed. My trust and hope is in the LORD.

I am like a tree planted by the waters, which spreads out its roots by the river.

In whatever situation I am in, I will not be afraid.

My life will always be green. I will not be anxious in difficult times and I will be fruitful all my life in Jesus name.

God's Divine Provision

DAY
13

Isaiah 66:9

"Shall I bring to the time of birth, and not cause delivery? says the LORD. "Shall I who cause delivery shut up the womb?" says your God."

I declare and decree in the name of Jesus Christ,

The LORD is my Provider.

The LORD who has created me will not abandon me.

The LORD who has made abundant provision for me will not forsake me.

Almighty God, you created me, kept me to this day; you will take care of all my needs and see me to the end in Jesus name.

God's Divine Provision

DAY
14

Isaiah 49:15-16

"Can a woman forget her nursing child, and not have compassion on the son of her womb? Surely they may forget, yet I will not forget you. See, I have inscribed you on the palms of My hands, your walls are continually before Me."

I declare and decree in the name of Jesus Christ,
The LORD is my Provider.
A woman can forget her nursing child and not have compassion on the son of her womb but my God will never forget me.
He has inscribed me on the palms of His hands.
My walls are continually before Him.
I am a very special child of God in Jesus name.

God's Divine Provision

DAY
15

1 Chronicles 4:10
"And Jabez called on the God of Israel saying, "Oh, that You would bless me indeed, and enlarge my territory, that Your hand would be with me, and that You would keep me from evil, that I may not cause pain!" So God granted him what he requested."

I declare and decree in the name of Jesus Christ,

The LORD is my Provider.

The LORD has blessed me and enlarged my territory.

The hand of God is with me.

He keeps me from evil.

I will not cause pain.

The LORD grants me my heart desire in Jesus name.

God's Divine Provision

DAY
16

Joel 2:25-26

"So I will restore to you the years that the swarming locust has eaten, the crawling locust, the consuming locust, and the chewing locust. My great army which I sent among you. You shall eat in plenty and be satisfied, and praise the name of the LORD your God, who has dealt wondrously with you and My people shall never be put to shame."

I declare and decree in the name of Jesus Christ,

The LORD is my Provider.

He has restored all that the swarming locust, the crawling locust, the consuming locust and the chewing locust has eaten.

I eat in plenty and I am satisfied.

I shall continually praise the name of the LORD. The LORD has dealt wondrously with me. I shall never be put to shame in Jesus name.

God's Divine Provision

DAY
17

Joel 2: 27

"Then you shall know that I am in the midst of Israel: I am the LORD your God and there is no other. My people shall never be put to shame."

I declare and decree in the name of Jesus Christ,

The LORD is my Provider.

The LORD is with me.

He is in the midst of my life.

He is the LORD my God and there is no other.

I shall never be put to shame.

I am covered with the glory of God in Jesus name.

God's Divine Provision

DAY
18

Isaiah 61:11

"For as the earth brings forth its bud. As the garden causes the things that are sown in it to spring forth, so the LORD GOD will cause righteousness and praise to spring forth before all the nations."

I declare and decree in the name of Jesus Christ,

The LORD is my Provider.

As the earth brings forth its bud,

as the garden causes the things that are sown in it to spring forth,

so the LORD GOD will cause righteousness (prosperity, justice)

and praise (celebration, glory, tehilla) to spring forth from my life before all the nations in Jesus name.

God's Divine Provision

DAY
19

Isaiah 3:10

"Say to the righteous that it shall be well with them, for they shall eat the fruit of their doings."

I declare and decree in the name of Jesus Christ,

The LORD is my Provider.

I am the righteousness of God through Jesus Christ.

It is well with me now.

It shall be well with me forever.

I shall eat the fruit of my doings in Jesus name.

God's Divine Provision

DAY
20

Proverbs 10:22
"The blessing of the LORD makes one rich and He adds no sorrow with it."

I declare and decree in the name of Jesus Christ,

The LORD is my Provider.

The blessing of the LORD makes me rich (grow).

He adds no sorrow with it.

I am blessed going out.

I am blessed coming in.

I am a channel of blessing in Jesus name.

God's Divine Provision

DAY
21

Deuteronomy 8:7
"For the LORD your God is bringing you into a good land, a land of brooks of water, of fountains and springs, that flow out of valleys and hills."

I declare and decree in the name of Jesus Christ,

The LORD is my Provider.

He has brought me into a good land.

It is a land of brooks of water.

I am living in a land of fountains and springs.

I am living in a land that flows out of valleys and hills.

My life is beautiful and blessed.

Glory be to God in Jesus name.

God's Divine Provision

DAY
22

Romans 8:32

"He who did not spare His own Son, but delivered Him up for us all, how shall He not with Him also freely give us all things?"

I declare and decree in the name of Jesus Christ,

The LORD is my Provider.

Almighty God, you did not spare your Son, my LORD Jesus Christ, but you delivered Him up for us all.

You are able to freely give me all things.

The heavens are open over me.

I receive all I need to reign and triumph as a child of God in Jesus name.

God's Divine Provision

DAY
23

Ezekiel 34:26

"I will make them and the places all around My hill a blessing; and I will cause showers to come down in their season, there shall be showers of blessing."

I declare and decree in the name of Jesus Christ,

The LORD is my Provider.

He has blessed me.

He has made me and all the places around me a blessing.

The LORD shall cause showers of blessing to rain down on me in their season.

There shall be showers of blessing upon my life in Jesus name.

God's Divine Provision

DAY
24

Psalm 34:10
"The young lions lack and suffer hunger, but those who seek the LORD shall not lack any good thing."

I declare and decree in the name of Jesus Christ,

The LORD is my Provider.

I am a child of the Most High God.

I seek the LORD with all my heart.

I shall not lack naturally.

I shall not lack spiritually.

I shall not lack any good thing.

I have in abundance all I need in Jesus name.

God's Divine Provision

John 16:24

**"Until now you have asked nothing in My name.
Ask, and you will receive, that your joy may be full."**

I declare and decree in the name of Jesus Christ,

The LORD is my Provider.

He provides all my needs.

I do not lack anything good.

I ask in the name of Jesus Christ for overflow, for open heaven and abundance for my natural and spiritual needs and I receive.

My joy is full in Jesus name.

God's Divine Provision

DAY
26

Exodus 3:21

"And I will give this people favor in the sight of the Egyptians, and it shall be, when you go, that you shall not go empty-handed."

I declare and decree in the name of Jesus Christ,

The LORD is my Provider.

I receive favour in the sight of God and in the sight of men.

There shall be no more fruitless effort in my life.

My life is filled with the goodness and love of God in Jesus name.

God's Divine Provision

1 Corinthians 2:9

"But as it is written: "Eye has not seen, nor ear heard, nor have entered into the heart of man the things which God has prepared for those who love Him"

I declare and decree in the name of Jesus Christ,

The LORD is my Provider.

Eye has not seen, ear has not heard nor has it entered into the heart of man the things which God has prepared for us who love Him.

LORD, you are my Father and I am your child. Thank you for all you have for me on earth, I receive them.

Thank you for all you have in store for me in heaven, I look forward to receiving them in Jesus name.

God's Divine Provision

Luke 12:24

"Consider the ravens, for they neither sow nor reap, which have neither storehouse nor barn, and God feeds them. Of how much more value are you than the birds?"

I declare and decree in the name of Jesus Christ,

The LORD is my Provider.

The ravens do not sow nor reap, neither do they have storehouse nor barn, yet God feeds them.

I am more valuable to God than the birds.

Almighty God, I believe and trust in you.

You are my great provider in Jesus name.

God's Divine Provision

Psalm 23:1-3
"The LORD is my shepherd; I shall not want. He makes me to lie down in green pastures; He leads me beside the still waters. He restores My soul; He leads me in the paths of righteousness For His name's sake.

I declare and decree in the name of Jesus Christ,

The LORD is my Provider.

The LORD is my shepherd, I have everything

I need.

He lets me rest in fields of green grass and leads me to quiet pools of fresh water.

He gives me new strength. He guides me in the right paths, as He has promised.

Glory be to your holy name in Jesus name.

God's Divine Provision

DAY
30

Hebrews 4:16

"Let us therefore come boldly to the throne of grace, that we may obtain mercy and find grace to help in time of need."

I declare and decree in the name of Jesus Christ,

The LORD is my Provider.

I come boldly to the throne of grace.

I obtain mercy and grace from God.

I obtain abundant mercy and grace to help me in time of need in Jesus name.

God's Divine Provision

DAY
31

2 Corinthians 9:8

"And God is able to make all grace abound toward you, that you, always having all sufficiency in all things, may have an abundance for every good work."

I declare and decree in the name of Jesus Christ,

The LORD is my Provider.

He makes His abundant grace abound towards me.

I have more than enough in all things, to care of my needs and to do God's work in Jesus name.

God's Divine Provision

Other books by the author:

I Know who I am in Christ Jesus
(Biblical Confessions for 365 Days)
Biblical Portrait of the Woman
(60 days scriptures for a Praying Woman)
God's Healing Promises
(31 days healing declarations)

Coming soon:

Total Deliverance (31 Days Scriptures for Total Deliverance)

God's Inner Peace (90 Days Scriptural Declarations of God's covenant of peace with me)

Living Under God's Covering (90 days biblical declarations for protection)

Exercising Divine Authority (90 days scriptural declarations for Healing, Provision & Deliverance)

Have you been blessed with our book(s)?
Do you have any suggestion or comment? We would love to hear from you.
Please contact us: joykent@declarehisword.com

God's Divine Provision

Note

God's Divine Provision

Note

God's Divine Provision

Note

God's Divine Provision

www.ingramcontent.com/pod-product-compliance
Lightning Source LLC
Chambersburg PA
CBHW020944160726
47993CB00007B/2925